A Gift For: Lucinda

From: Rosine

x

July 2003

BEST FRIENDS

a photographic celebration

BOK4034

Friendship

is precious,

not only in

the shade,

but in the

sunshine of life.

President Thomas Jefferson

Friendship needs no words.

Dag Hammarskjöld

The happiest business in all the world

is that of making friends.

Anne S. Eaton

Friendship is love without wings.

Lord Byron

Friendship

is the source of

the greatest pleasures,

and without friends even the

most agreeable pursuits

become tedious.

St. Thomas Aquinas

A friend is a present which you give yourself.

Robert Louis Stevenson

There's nothing

worth the wear

of winning,

But laughter and

the love of friends.

Hilaire Belloc

Good friendships are fragile things and require as much care as any other fragile and precious things.

Randolph Bourne

We are so

fond of one

another

because our

ailments are

the same.

Jonathan Swift

A true friend is the most precious of all possessions

and the one we take least thought about acquiring.

La Rochefoucauld

When the chips are not

exactly down but just

scattered about, you

discover who your real

friends are.

Richard Burton

I have no talent for making new friends

but oh such genius for fidelity to old ones.

Daphne du Maurier

Good friends are

good for your health.

Dr. Irwin Sarason

Nothing can come between

true friends.

Euripides

Treat your friends as you do pictures,

and place them in their best light.

Jennie Jerome Churchill

Never explain: your friends

don't need it and your

enemies won't believe it.

Victor Grayson

Give me one friend, just one,

who meets the needs of

all my varying moods.

Esther M. Clark

Love is only chatter

Friends are all that matter.

Gelett Burgess

When

a friend

speaks to me,

whatever he says

is interesting.

Jean Renoir

We cherish our friends

not for their ability to amuse us,

but for ours to be amused by them.

Evelyn Waugh

No man is the whole of himself.

His friends are the rest of him.

from the "Good Life Almanac"

There is nothing of this earth

more proved than true friendship.

St. Thomas Aquinas

Friendships last when each friend

thinks he has a slight superiority over the other.

Anonymous

…a good friend is the purest of all God's gifts,

for it is a love that has no exchange of payment.

Frances Farmer

I think this is

the beginning

of a beautiful

friendship.

from the film "Casablanca"

The growth

of friendship

may be a

lifelong affair.

Sarah Orne Jewett

Life is to be

fortified by many friendships.

To love and be loved,

is the greatest happiness

of existence.

Sydney Smith

I am a hoarder of

two things: documents

and trusted friends.

Muriel Spark

Happy the man

who finds a generous friend.

Greek Proverb

Friends are born,

not made.

Henry Brooks Adams

The older the friend the better.

Plautus

However rare true love is,

true friendship is rarer.

La Rochefoucauld

But every road is rough to me

That has no friend to cheer it.

Elizabeth Shane

The only reward

of virtue is virtue;

the only way to

have a friend is

to be one.

Ralph Waldo Emerson

Most people

enjoy the

inferiority

of their

best friends.

Lord Chesterfield

We have

such a friendship

that is given to very few.

Bette Davis

Friendship is one heart

in two bodies.

Joseph Zabara

Your friend is the man who knows all about you

and still likes you.

Elbert Hubbard

I always felt that the great high privilege,

relief and comfort of friendship was that

one had to explain nothing.

Katherine Mansfield

A friend is a person

with whom I may be

sincere. Before him I

may think aloud.

Ralph Waldo Emerson

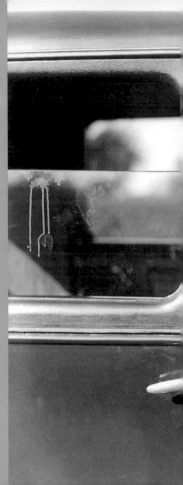

Happiness seems made to be shared.

Jean Racine

True Happiness

consists not in the multitude of friends,

But in the worth and choice.

Ben Jonson

Advice from friends

is like the weather;

some of it is good;

some of it is bad.

Arnold Lobel

Many a friendship, long, loyal and

self-sacrificing, rests on no thicker

a foundation than a kind word.

Frederick W. Faber

A friend is someone who understands your past,

believes in your future and accepts you today

just the way you are.

Proverbs 27:17

The friendships which last are those wherein each friend respects the other's dignity to the point of not really wanting anything from him.

Cyril Connolly

Friendship is honey – but don't eat it all.

Moroccan Proverb

To like and

dislike the

same things,

that is

indeed true

friendship.

Sallust

I no doubt deserved my enemies, but I don't believe I deserved my friends.

Walt Whitman

The greatest gift of life

is friendship.

Hubert Horatio Humphrey

And we find at the end of a perfect day

The soul of a friend we've made.

Carrie Jacobs Bond

There is no wilderness like life without friends; friendship multiplies blessings and minimises misfortunes; it is a unique remedy against adversity and it soothes the soul.

Baltasar

Don't walk in front of me,

I may not follow.

Don't walk behind me,

I may not lead.

Walk beside me,

And just be my friend.

Anonymous

Picture Credits

All images Hulton Getty Picture Collection.

cover: Old ladies in Jacobean dress, Norfolk, UK, 1929.

title page: George Spinney with his bulldog at a dog show, Crystal Palace, London, UK, 1926.

page 4/5: Three women enjoy a riverside picnic, 1937.

page 7: A dog joins three people gazing at a stormy Herne Bay, UK, 1934.

page 8: Two girls at the Mobile County Rural Center, Mount Vernon, Alabama, US, 1956.

page 10/11: A Canadian soldier recuperating at an English coastal resort, with the help of two female friends, 1940.

page 12: Enjoying candy floss at a fun fair, Battersea Park, London, UK, 1953.

page 15: Young holidaymakers paddling at Viking Bay, Broadstairs, UK, 1927.

page 16/17: Women taking part in a laughing competition, Sandown, Isle of Wight, UK, 1933.

page 19: Daphne and Tony Beacon playing a game of hide-and-seek, Hyde Park, London, UK, 1931.

page 20/21: Two women gossiping during an interval in the band music, Hyde Park, London, UK, 1939.

page 22: Two young bathers, Shanklin, Isle of Wight, UK, circa 1940.

page 24/25: As title page.

page 27: Residents of the Bishopswood Home in Highgate, London, UK, chat over a cup of tea, 1943.

page 29: A game of leapfrog on the beach, 1955.

page 31: A young boy asleep with his dog, circa 1955.

page 32/33: Two women enjoy tea in the sunshine on the high diving board at Finchley open air baths, London, UK, 1938.

page 35: A New York street gang brag about their exploits to a potential new recruit, circa 1955.

page 36: Two young women enjoy a summer day on Blackpool promenade, UK, 1951.

page 38: Cocktails aboard the S S Chusan cruise liner off the coast of Norway, 1951.

page 40: A quiet chat in a Cornish village, 1938.

page 43: A young woman leaps to join her friends in a rowing boat, circa 1950.

page 45: Two elderly Dutch men, circa 1950.

page 47: School friends, London, UK, 1934.

page 48: A boxer dog and baby exchange looks, circa 1955.

page 51: Two "Miss World" contestants, 1953.

page 52/53: Circus elephants pop their trunks through a tent opening, 1937.

page 54/55: A school boy pushes his friend on his new

"Roadracer" go-cart, 1947.

page 57: Eight unemployed Welsh girls, who have trained to be West End Mannequins at Lucie Clayton's modeling school, 1937.

page 58/59: British Legion members enjoying a cup of tea in Kensington Gardens, London, UK, 1971.

page 61: Children playing by a stream in the Scottish countryside, 1954.

page 62/53: Twins Pauline and Pamela Chamberlain, aged five 1938.

page 65: Two elderly women on a cobbled street in Polperro, Cornwall, UK, 1938.

page 66: Peter Wiess and his Manchester terrier, Tiny, exploring the edge of the lake at Battersea Park, London, UK, 1949.

page 68/69: Revellers on new year's eve in Times Square, New York 1962. © Ernst Haas courtesy Hulton Getty, Picture Collection.

page 70: Two boys in a London street, UK, 1954.

page 72/73: Baron the chimpanzee enjoys a ride in Carl Detroy's toy car, London, Essex, UK, 1949.

page 74/75: Easter holiday campers at Field-Common farm, England, 1932.

page 77: Two school friends, Petersham, UK, 1910.

page 78: An old man and porcupine share a moment of affection, circa 1955.

page 81: A ladies hairdressing salon set up in the street to take advantage of fine weather, 1975.

page 82/83: Bloodhounds in a car during bloodhound trials at Aston Abbots, Buckinghamshire, UK, 1933.

page 85: Balancing on the beach, circa 1955.

page 86: A young boy mimics the stance of the men he is following, 1972.

page 88/89: Ladies take tea in the rain at the "Nature Flower Show", Chelsea, London, UK, 1980.

page 93: The Good queue on a visit to a farm in Bristol, UK, 1954.

page 94/95: A conversation at the "Grandfathers' Club" at Elephant and Castle, south London, UK, 1949.

page 97: Two ladies enjoying a picnic, Bournemouth, UK, 1930.

page 99: Playing a board game at the Mobile County Rural Center, Mount Vernon, Alabama, US, circa 1956.

page 100: Checking the mail box, 1955.

page 102/03: Amish schoolboys, circa 1956.

page 105: Participants in the "Holiday Girl Beauty Competition" asleep on one of the beds at the Royal Pavilion in Brighton, UK, 1953.

page 107: Enjoying the autumn sun on the banks of a German lake, 1957.

page 108: Two young boys stop for a chat on a deserted Copacabana beach, 1967

Copyright © 2001 by MQ Publications Limited

This edition published in 2001 by MQ Publications exclusively for Hallmark Cards, Inc.

www.hallmark.com

Printed and bound in China

6 7 8 9 10

Cover design: John Casey
Design: WDA
Text and picture research: Suzie Green
Series Editor: Elizabeth Carr